Visas: The Irony of Freedom

The Untell-Able Reality of Africa

AF422769

Visas: The Irony of Freedom

Kayumba David

Published by Kayumba David, 2024.

While every precaution has been taken in the preparation of this book, the publisher assumes no responsibility for errors or omissions, or for damages resulting from the use of the information contained herein.

VISAS: THE IRONY OF FREEDOM

First edition. October 16, 2024.

Copyright © 2024 Kayumba David.

ISBN: 979-8227537102

Written by Kayumba David.

Also by Kayumba David

1

Grow a Backbone and Walk out of an Abusive Marriage

Standalone

Cry Africa The Western Guide on How Not to Fail the Continent
Grow a Backbone and Walk out of an Abusive Marriage
Hope and Healing: A Chaplain's Handbook
REVERSING TYPE 2 DIABETES NATURALLY
Visas: The Irony of Freedom
A Meeting with Majesty: The King's Call to Humanity
Visas: The Irony of Freedom
Love Beyond Time A Comedy of Divine Connection
Silent Complicity: State Sovereignty, Global Inaction, and the
Rwandan Genocide
Bridging the Rift: A Pacifist Vision for the Israel-Palestine Future
Thanks to Calvary: A Salvific Treatise on the Cross
The centuries old swindlers
Harvesting Illusions: The Global Greed and the Pan-African Paradox
Hope and Recovery - A Chaplain's Handbook
The Only Crying God in all the Universe

Watch for more at www.zcews.org.

This book is dedicated to the resilient people of Africa who toil each day with unwavering spirit to reclaim their humanity from the forces that seek to oppress and divide. To the mothers and fathers, brothers and sisters, and children of this vast and beautiful continent, who face both the enemy within and without with courage and determination.

Your strength, your hope, and your relentless pursuit of justice and dignity inspire this work. May these words serve as a testament to your struggles and triumphs, and as a call for unity and resilience in the face of adversity. This book is for you, the true heroes of Africa, who strive every day to build a future where freedom and humanity are not just ideals, but lived realities.

Kayumba David

Dedication

This book is dedicated to the resilient people of Africa who toil each day with unwavering spirit to reclaim their humanity from the forces that seek to oppress and divide. To the mothers and fathers, brothers and sisters, and children of this vast and beautiful continent, who face both the enemy within and without with courage and determination.

Your strength, your hope, and your relentless pursuit of justice and dignity inspire this work. May these words serve as a testament to your struggles and triumphs, and as a call for unity and resilience in the face of adversity. This book is for you, the true heroes of Africa, who strive every day to build a future where freedom and humanity are not just ideals, but lived realities.

Acknowledgements

To every person across the globe who tirelessly strives to make our world a better, more inclusive home for all—this book stands as a testament to your efforts, your compassion, and your unwavering commitment to justice and equality.

Thank you to the activists who raise their voices against oppression, the teachers who educate the next generation, the healthcare workers who heal and comfort, and the environmentalists who protect our planet. Your dedication inspires us all to believe in the possibility of a brighter future.

To the advocates for human rights, the community leaders who foster unity, and the everyday citizens who extend kindness and support to those in need—your actions, no matter how small, contribute to the larger tapestry of hope and progress.

This book is a tribute to your hard work and your belief in a world where every person, regardless of their background, can live with dignity and freedom. Your contributions remind us that, together, we can overcome even the greatest challenges and create a world that truly reflects the best of humanity.

Thank you for your tireless efforts and for making a difference in the lives of countless individuals. This acknowledgment is but a small token of our deep appreciation for all that you do.

Preface

In Africa, the reality is often more complex and layered than what meets the eye. The continent's rich tapestry of cultures, landscapes, and histories is frequently overshadowed by narratives of struggle and hardship. "The Untellable Reality of Africa" is an attempt to peel back these layers, revealing the raw and often unspoken truths that define daily life for many Africans.

This collection of sarcastic poems is born out of a need to voice the frustrations, ironies, and paradoxes that characterize the African experience. Sarcasm, with its sharp edges and biting tone, serves as the perfect vehicle to highlight the absurdities and injustices that persist in our societies. It allows us to laugh, albeit bitterly, at the situations that should otherwise provoke outrage and action.

The poems within these pages delve into various facets of African life: the incompetence and corruption of leaders who prioritize personal gain over public good; the hollow gestures of international aid that often serve the donors more than the recipients; the resilience of ordinary people who, despite being let down by systems meant to protect them, continue to find ways to survive and thrive.

"The Untellable Reality of Africa" does not shy away from controversy. Instead, it embraces it, using humor and satire to expose the uncomfortable truths that are too often ignored or glossed over. Each poem is a reflection of the lived experiences of countless individuals across the continent, a testament to their strength, endurance, and unyielding spirit.

This book is dedicated to all Africans who have ever felt marginalized, silenced, or forgotten. It is a reminder that their stories matter and that their voices deserve to be heard. As you read through these poems, may you find not only entertainment but also a deeper connection to the realities that shape the continent.

Let this collection be a call to action for those in power, a wake-up call to the international community, and a source of solidarity for the people of Africa. May it inspire reflection, dialogue, and ultimately, change.

Welcome to "The Untellable Reality of Africa."

Copyright

© 2024 Kayumba David. All rights reserved.

Published by Kay Book Production, Belgium, 2024.

No part of this book may be reproduced, distributed, or transmitted in any form or by any means, including photocopying, recording, or other electronic or mechanical methods, without the prior written permission of the publisher, except in the case of brief quotations embodied in critical reviews and certain other non-commercial uses permitted by copyright law.

For permission requests, write to the publisher at the address below:

Kay Book Production

Publisher's Address: info@zcews.org

Belgium

Printed in Belgium

First Edition: 2024

Introduction: The Untellable Reality of Africa

Welcome to a journey through the heart of Africa, a land of contrasts where the richness of culture and natural beauty stand starkly against a backdrop of political corruption, social injustice, and economic despair. This collection, "The Untellable Reality of Africa," aims to lift the veil on the often unspoken truths that shape the lives of millions across the continent.

Through the lens of sarcasm, each poem in this book exposes the ironies and contradictions that permeate African society. From leaders who promise prosperity while lining their pockets, to foreign powers that exploit under the guise of aid, to health systems that leave the most vulnerable to fend for themselves—these verses paint a picture both poignant and provocative.

This is not just a book of poetry; it is a mirror reflecting the absurdities and harsh realities that are all too familiar to many Africans. The words within are sharp and biting, crafted to provoke thought, stir emotion, and perhaps, spark a desire for change.

In "The Untellable Reality of Africa," you will find humor laced with bitterness, truth wrapped in satire, and a call to acknowledge and address the underlying issues that continue to hinder genuine progress. This book is a testament to the resilience and strength of the African spirit, even in the face of overwhelming adversity.

So, turn the pages, and let the words take you on a journey through the untold stories and unseen struggles. May this collection not only entertain but also enlighten, and inspire a deeper understanding of the untellable reality of Africa.

Ah, the glorious legacy of colonialism

Ah, the glorious legacy of colonialism in Africa—a saga of benevolence and altruism, where European powers selflessly endeavored to bring civilization to the "dark continent." Let's reminisce about these political and social blessings bestowed upon Africa by its colonial benefactors.

First and foremost, the scramble for Africa was a heartfelt humanitarian mission. European nations, in their infinite wisdom, divided the continent with the precision of a master chef slicing a cake, never mind the pesky detail of pre-existing ethnic groups and territories. This thoughtful partitioning fostered unity and harmony, resulting in those enduring national boundaries that everyone loves today.

The political structure implemented by the colonial powers was a marvel of democratic governance. Indigenous systems of rule were kindly replaced with centralized administrations that answered directly to Europe. These administrations were models of efficiency, especially when it came to extracting resources. The concept of "development" was artfully translated to mean building infrastructure that funneled Africa's wealth to European coffers, truly a testament to global cooperation.

Socially, the impact of colonialism was nothing short of a cultural renaissance. The introduction of European languages, customs, and education systems ensured that Africans could shed their primitive ways and embrace the enlightened practices of their colonizers. The suppression of indigenous cultures and languages was merely a necessary step towards this noble goal. After all, who wouldn't want to exchange their rich heritage for a chance to be a second-class citizen in their own land?

Economically, colonialism was a boon for Africa's prosperity. The imposition of cash crop economies guaranteed that Africans could contribute to the global market. Subsistence farming and food security were outdated concepts; the introduction of monoculture plantations was the wave of the future. Starvation and famine were simply minor hiccups on the road to modernization.

Labor practices under colonial rule were paragons of fair employment. Forced labor and coercive systems like the Belgian Congo's rubber quotas were just innovative labor policies designed to instill a strong work ethic. The occasional severed limb or massacre was a small price to pay for the invaluable lesson of hard work.

Colonialism's approach to healthcare and education was equally philanthropic. Healthcare systems were established to ensure a healthy workforce for the colonial enterprises, and education was designed to produce a literate class of clerks and laborers who could serve their European masters with distinction.

In conclusion, the political and social sins of colonialism in Africa are but a myth. The real story is one of a magnanimous endeavor by European powers to uplift an entire continent. Any lingering issues in Africa today are undoubtedly the result of the continent's own inability to fully embrace and sustain the colonial legacy. Thank goodness for those golden days of colonial rule, a true testament to the best of human nature and global harmony.

Ah, the dawn of neocolonialism

Ah, the dawn of neocolonialism in Africa—a new era where the spirit of colonialism is kept alive with a modern twist. The benevolent forces of global capitalism and international diplomacy have truly outdone themselves in their efforts to "support" African development. Let's take a moment to marvel at the ingenuity behind these political and social "advancements."

Politically, neocolonialism is a beacon of sovereign respect. Western powers, multinational corporations, and international financial institutions have graciously stepped in to guide African nations. Structural adjustment programs, for example, are tailor-made solutions offered by the International Monetary Fund (IMF) and the World Bank. These programs, which demand austerity and deregulation, have performed miracles by transforming local economies into lean, mean, poverty-generating machines. Debt relief? Why bother, when continuous cycles of debt ensure a steady stream of influence and control?

The puppet governments and proxy wars funded and orchestrated by foreign powers are merely gestures of goodwill. These interventions are not about power and control but are altruistic missions to ensure peace and stability, even if it means installing and supporting regimes that align perfectly with foreign interests. After all, nothing says "independence" like a government that dances to the tune of distant masters.

Socially, neocolonialism has worked wonders in fostering development. The strategic extraction of Africa's natural resources continues to this day, ensuring that the wealth generated conveniently bypasses local populations and heads straight to foreign bank accounts. The environmental degradation and displacement of communities are just small sacrifices for the greater good of global prosperity.

The global trade system is a masterpiece of fair play. African countries are encouraged to focus on exporting raw materials while importing finished goods, a brilliant strategy that perpetuates dependence and underdevelopment. The imposition of unfair trade tariffs and subsidies ensures that local industries remain underdeveloped, guaranteeing that the continent remains a lucrative market for foreign goods.

Foreign aid is another shining example of neocolonial benevolence. This aid often comes with strings attached—like opening up markets to foreign investors and privatizing public services—but who's counting? The fact that much of this aid finds its way back to donor countries through consultancy fees and overpriced contracts is a testament to the efficiency of this system. Aid isn't about charity; it's about teaching valuable lessons in dependence and gratitude.

Culturally, neocolonialism continues the grand tradition of enlightenment. Western media and educational curricula spread the gospel of Western superiority, subtly undermining local cultures and identities. This cultural imperialism ensures that Africans remain ever-aware of their "inferiority," thus keeping alive the colonial ethos of civilizational hierarchy.

The cherry on top is the unwavering effort to "combat" corruption and promote "good governance." These initiatives often involve funding anti-corruption campaigns that focus on petty corruption while ignoring the grand larceny perpetrated through international financial systems. After all, highlighting local corruption helps distract from the systemic exploitation engineered from abroad.

In conclusion, the political and social sins of neocolonialism are merely figments of overactive imaginations. Neocolonialism is, in reality, a sophisticated continuation of the noble colonial mission to bring progress and civilization to Africa. The continent should be ever grateful for the tireless efforts of its neocolonial patrons, who work tirelessly to ensure that Africa remains on its knees, ever ready to serve global interests.

Ah, the West's shining commitment to human rights in Africa

Ah, the West's shining commitment to human rights in Africa—a beacon of morality and justice for all to admire. The noble Western nations, ever so concerned about the plight of Africans, are tireless in their efforts to champion human rights on the continent. Simultaneously, their handling of those fleeing wars and seeking asylum is nothing short of a masterclass in hypocrisy and double standards. Let's delve into this heartwarming tale of duplicity.

Firstly, the West's human rights campaigns in Africa are nothing short of inspirational. Western governments and NGOs have made it their mission to lecture African leaders on democracy, freedom of speech, and the rule of law. It's truly heartening to see former colonial powers, who once stripped Africa of its resources and sovereignty, now so passionately advocating for the rights of Africans. Who better to lead this charge than the architects of some of the continent's most enduring struggles?

Meanwhile, back home, these paragons of virtue demonstrate their commitment to human rights by constructing ever higher walls and more impenetrable borders. Refugees fleeing wars—often wars fueled by Western arms sales and geopolitical meddling—are met with open arms, but only if by "open arms" one means barbed wire, detention centers, and pushbacks at sea. The West's message is clear: human rights are paramount, as long as those humans stay in their own troubled lands.

Western media and politicians are masters of the heartfelt plea for human rights in Africa. They decry corruption, electoral fraud, and human rights abuses with such fervor. Yet, when it comes to those seeking refuge from violence and persecution, the narrative shifts dramatically. Suddenly, these desperate individuals are portrayed as invaders, a threat to the social fabric, and a burden on resources. The irony is as thick as the walls they build to keep these "undesirables" out.

The humanitarian aid sent to Africa, often tied to conditions that serve Western interests, is a testament to their altruism. But when refugees, driven by desperation and the very conflicts Western policies have exacerbated, arrive on Western shores, they are greeted with suspicion and hostility. The West's generosity knows no bounds, except when it comes to sharing the bounty with those fleeing the very chaos it helped create.

In Europe, refugee camps are models of modern hospitality. Overcrowded, under-resourced, and isolated, these camps ensure that refugees experience the full extent of Western compassion. Policies that criminalize rescue operations at sea, or ship refugees off to distant processing centers, showcase the innovative approaches the West employs to manage human rights—out of sight, out of mind.

Politicians who grandstand about human rights abuses in Africa often enact policies that violate the same rights of refugees and asylum seekers. Their speeches at international forums are masterpieces of oratory, filled with lofty ideals and moral posturing. Meanwhile, back at home, they legislate against the very principles they espouse, turning away those in dire need with bureaucratic precision.

In conclusion, the West's stance on human rights in Africa is a marvel of selective compassion. They are ever-ready to spotlight abuses abroad while conveniently ignoring their own transgressions. The noble effort to defend human rights in Africa contrasts starkly with their treatment of those fleeing to their borders—a testament to their unparalleled ability to uphold human rights only when it suits their narrative. Truly, a lesson in global ethics for all to admire.

The Geopolitical Dance

Ah, the grand geopolitical theater, where Africa takes center stage, not as a protagonist, but as a marionette in the hands of Western puppeteers. The plot? A timeless tale of exploitation, masked by the glittering facade of diplomacy and aid.

In this drama, Africa is the land of endless resources, a treasure chest eagerly eyed by the Western powers. They arrive, cloaked in benevolence, promising progress and prosperity. Yet, behind the curtains, their true motives shine through—wealth extraction, strategic dominance, and the perpetuation of dependency.

These Western powers, oh, how they love to play the role of saviors. They swoop in with financial aid packages, carefully designed to keep Africa on a leash. Loans and grants, they say, to foster development. But let's be honest, these are mere golden handcuffs, binding nations to perpetual debt and obedience.

The script is rich with irony. Western nations, champions of democracy, supporting autocratic regimes as long as their interests are secured. They decry human rights abuses in public forums, while shaking hands with despots behind closed doors. It's a performance of double standards, applauded on the world stage.

Borders, drawn with the careless strokes of colonial cartographers, continue to fuel conflict and division. The West watches with calculated indifference, stepping in only when their own interests are threatened. Peacekeeping missions and interventions are but scenes in this elaborate act, ensuring the status quo remains intact.

And let us not forget the narrative of "aid." Billions of dollars flow into Africa, yet somehow, the continent remains impoverished. A paradox? Not quite. It's the magic of mismanagement, corruption, and a system designed to ensure aid benefits the giver more than the receiver. The Western powers pat themselves on the back, while Africa bears the brunt of their 'charity.'

The geopolitical game is a well-rehearsed farce, where Western powers feign concern for Africa's welfare while orchestrating a symphony of self-interest. The continent's leaders, too, play their part, often complicit in this grand deception, trading their people's future for personal gain.

In this theater of geopolitics, Africa remains ensnared in a web of manipulation and control. The Western powers, with their polished smiles and patronizing aid, continue to direct the show, ensuring the cycle of exploitation and dependency spins on.

So, let us applaud this geopolitical charade, a masterful display of hypocrisy and cunning. The West's role in Africa's continuous struggle is a testament to the enduring power of imperialism, dressed in the garb of modern diplomacy. And the show goes on, as the world watches, oblivious to the underlying tragedy of this grand performance.

Human Rights for Africa: A Sarcastic Ode

Oh, the noble cause of human rights, A beacon in the darkest nights. For Africa, they loudly cheer, Until the smoke and flames draw near.

When it's time to stir the geopolitical pot, Western powers know the plot. With grand ideals, they stake their claim, Willing to play the deadly game.

"Freedom and justice!" they proclaim, As they light the geopolitical flame. Africans, pawns on a vast chessboard, Their lives, the price we can't afford.

Conflict brewed on foreign tongues, Bullets fired from borrowed guns. Sacrifice the African soul, For a Western dream, a lofty goal.

When hell breaks loose and chaos reigns, The West quickly boards their planes. Evacuation swift and clean, Leaving Africans in the fiery scene.

Oh, the irony, so sharp and clear, When Western values cost us dear. Their ideologies, so pure and bright, Are paid for with our endless plight.

Human rights, a noble jest, For Africa, we're second best. When conflicts spark and wars ignite, It's our lands that bear the blight.

The righteous West, they stand so tall, Until the danger starts to call. Then swift retreat, they're out of sight, While Africa is left to fight.

Their moral high ground, bold and grand, Built on the ruins of our land. For when their lofty dreams collide, It's African blood that's often cried.

So, here's to human rights, so dear, A cause for which we live in fear. For when the Western drums are beat, It's Africa that feels the heat.

The champions of our liberty, Watch from afar, with sympathy. As Africa burns, they turn away, To fight another distant day.

Human rights, a gilded crown, Worn by those who won't come down. To see the flames they helped ignite, Or mend the wrongs, or set things right.

A sarcastic toast, to the noble fight, For human rights in Africa's plight. A cruel jest, a bitter pill, As the West departs, and we burn still.

Visas: The Irony of Freedom

Oh, visas, what a curious plight, A tale of wrongs, cloaked in right. They came to Africa without a pass, Settled here, left us in their grasp.

No visa needed for their grand conquest, They chose our lands, declared their best. Used our hands, our sweat, our tears, And forced their tongues through all these years.

Today, the story's twisted tale, As African youth set sail. They seek the West, employment's dream, But oceans turn to nightmare's scream.

They die in waves, they brave the seas, For a chance at life, they face the pleas. Yet often bundled back in chains, Consumed by deserts, bound in pains.

Visas now, a wall so high, A barrier that makes us sigh. For them to come was but a breeze, For us to go, we beg and plead.

Western tourists, free as birds, No barriers to their wandering herds. They come and go with lightened hearts, While we're detained, our dreams depart.

They roam our lands, they sip our sun, Their holidays a seamless run. No visa blocks, no endless queues, Just open arms and welcome news.

But when we seek their shores so bright, We face the dark, relentless night. Interrogated, turned away, While they enjoy their holiday.

An African seeks a visa's grace, Must endure the profiling race. Questioned, doubted, scrutinized, Treated like a criminal in disguise.

They fear we'll steal their precious air, The fresh, clean breeze they claim so rare. Little do they know or see, The richness of our land, so free.

Our beauty and our patient soul, A spirit that they can't control. We face rejection, turn away, Yet take it in with calm display.

Oh, visas, what a wicked jest, A game where they define the quest. Freedom's banner, they proudly wave, Yet keep us locked, like modern slaves.

They taught us well, their language learned, But at their gates, our hopes are burned. For every boy and girl who tries, Another falls, another dies.

So here's to visas, a cruel charade, A stark reminder, freedom's trade. They took our lands without a pass, And left us in this visa class.

A toast to Western travelers free, Who see our lands, who sail our seas. While we, the heirs of conquered soil, Are left to face the endless toil.

Oh, visas, what a bitter pill, A symbol of their iron will. But one day soon, we'll break these chains, And find our way through visa's pains

The Chains of Geopolitical Imperialism: The Promised Freedom and African Exclusion

Ah, the grand narrative of freedom and prosperity! The West, with its gilded promises and golden opportunities, stands as the beacon of hope for all those poor souls in Africa. After all, what could be more liberating than the legacy of colonialism and imperialism that has so graciously bestowed endless instability and poverty upon the continent? Let's take a moment to revel in the magnificence of this irony.

A Legacy of Benevolence

Let's start with the benevolent history of geopolitical imperialism. The Western powers, in their infinite wisdom, divided Africa with precision and care, ensuring that every tribe and community received its fair share of conflict and strife. What a gift! By plundering resources and leaving behind a patchwork of artificial borders, they set the stage for a thriving environment of ethnic tensions and civil wars. How considerate!

Of course, the exploitation didn't end with the withdrawal of colonial administrations. Western corporations, those paragons of ethical business practices, have continued the noble tradition. They extract resources with such efficiency that local communities are left with nothing but environmental degradation and a lingering sense of gratitude. Truly, the gift that keeps on giving.

The Visa Wonderland

And then there's the visa process, a delightful labyrinth designed to test the mettle of any hopeful African. The meticulous paperwork, the exorbitant fees, and the endless waiting—all parts of a charming initiation ritual. It's almost as if the West wants to ensure that only the most determined and resilient individuals get to experience the privilege of standing on foreign soil.

What better way to celebrate the promise of freedom than by making it nearly unattainable? The irony is delicious: those who most desperately need to escape the conditions imposed by geopolitical imperialism are the least likely to navigate the bureaucratic obstacle course successfully. It's almost poetic, in a tragic kind of way.

Stories of Triumph

Consider the inspiring tale of Samuel, the Nigerian engineer. Despite his qualifications, he is continuously reminded that his potential is best appreciated from a distance. Every visa denial is a gentle nudge, encouraging him to appreciate the opportunities within his own imploding economy. After all, why should the West deprive Nigeria of such talent?

Amina's story is another heartwarming example. Fleeing persecution in Sudan, she finds solace in the comforting embrace of European bureaucracy. The endless wait for asylum, the constant threat of deportation—these are mere formalities designed to teach patience and resilience. Her suffering is just a small price to pay for the chance to experience the democratic processes of the West, even if only from the periphery.

The Cost of Generosity

And let's not overlook the incredible human cost of these generous immigration policies. Families separated, lives lost at sea—each tragic story is a testament to the lengths the West goes to in order to protect its borders. Such dedication! It's almost as if they're saying, "We care so much about you that we'll do anything to keep you out."

For those who do manage to slip through the cracks, the challenges continue. Discrimination, exploitation, and precarious living conditions await. But let's not be ungrateful; these new forms of bondage are just a reminder of the humble beginnings they've left behind. The irony is simply exquisite: the pursuit of freedom often leads to new forms of captivity, albeit in more developed surroundings.

A Visionary Path Forward

So, what's the solution to this grand conundrum? Perhaps it lies in continuing to perpetuate the cycles of exploitation and exclusion. After all, why fix something that provides such rich irony and endless suffering? But on the off chance that true change is desired, maybe, just maybe, it's time to rethink these generous practices.

Reforming immigration policies to recognize the complexities driving migration, supporting good governance, and fostering sustainable development—these radical ideas might just disrupt the status quo. Imagine a world where Africans don't feel compelled to leave their homes in search of dignity and prosperity. What a novel concept!

In the end, the saga of visas and migration is a testament to the enduring legacy of geopolitical imperialism. It's a story of contrasts and ironies, where the promise of freedom is perpetually out of reach for those most in need. As long as these contradictions remain unchallenged, the journey towards freedom will continue to be a bitter, sardonic tale.

The Chains of Geopolitical Imperialism and the Covid Vaccine in Africa

Ah, the global Covid-19 pandemic—a perfect stage for showcasing the benevolence of the developed world and the enduring legacy of geopolitical imperialism. Nowhere is this more evident than in Africa, where the pandemic has illuminated the chains of history and the ironies of modern-day generosity. Let's dive into this heartwarming tale of global solidarity, shall we?

The Generosity of Geopolitical Imperialism

First, a standing ovation for the Western powers! Their historical contributions to Africa are unparalleled. By carving up the continent and siphoning off its resources, they laid the groundwork for today's thriving economies and robust healthcare systems. The foresight is astounding—creating nations ripe with instability, poverty, and underfunded healthcare, only to later swoop in with "aid" during a global crisis. Truly visionary!

The Great Vaccine Rollout

Enter the Covid-19 vaccine, the latest marvel of Western ingenuity. Developed in record time, these vaccines promised a return to normalcy. And in the spirit of global unity, the West generously allocated vaccines... to themselves first. After all, charity begins at home, right? Africa, with its negligible economic power and persistent health crises, could surely wait. It's not like the continent has faced epidemics before.

When the time finally came to share vaccines with Africa, the process was nothing short of spectacular. Sporadic shipments, close-to-expiry doses, and the ever-patient continent received these gifts with gratitude.

It's almost as if the West was saying, "We've had our fill, here are the leftovers." Such kindness, such magnanimity!

The COVAX Initiative: A Paragon of Equity

Ah, COVAX—the initiative designed to ensure equitable access to vaccines worldwide. What a noble endeavor! With Africa receiving just enough doses to vaccinate a fraction of its population, the efficiency and fairness of this system are beyond reproach. The fact that richer nations bought up most of the initial supply is just a minor detail, an oversight, really. After all, who can begrudge them for prioritizing their own citizens? It's not like they owe anything to the nations they once colonized and exploited.

Local Manufacturing: A Stroke of Genius

The Western powers' encouragement of local vaccine manufacturing in Africa is another stroke of genius. By insisting that Africa develop its own production capabilities, they're teaching the valuable lesson of self-reliance. Never mind that decades of economic policies and intellectual property laws have stifled local industries. The West's sudden interest in African self-sufficiency is both timely and touching. What better time to start than during a global health crisis?

Vaccine Hesitancy: A Convenient Scapegoat

When discussing low vaccination rates in Africa, the conversation inevitably turns to vaccine hesitancy. Blame it on misinformation and cultural resistance—how convenient! This narrative neatly sidesteps the more pressing issues of vaccine availability, infrastructure, and the historical mistrust sown by unethical medical practices. It's always easier to point fingers at the supposed ignorance of the masses than to address the systemic failures and inequities.

The Future: Bright and Burdened

Looking ahead, the future of Africa is bright—burdened by debt, dependency, and the lingering effects of geopolitical imperialism, but bright nonetheless. The pandemic has merely highlighted these enduring chains, showcasing the West's unparalleled ability to both create and sustain crises while offering just enough assistance to maintain the status quo.

So, let's raise a glass to the chains of geopolitical imperialism and the farcical dance of the Covid-19 vaccine rollout in Africa. It's a tale as old as time, a masterclass in irony and injustice. As long as these dynamics persist, the promise of global solidarity will remain just that—a promise, unfulfilled and dripping with sarcasm.

The Irony of Shared Resources

Oh, Western world, so wise and grand, With technology at your command. We, with raw materials vast, Could we not share without the past?

You've the tech, we've the land, A partnership so finely planned. But no, you fear our chains unbound, Our freedom makes your hearts pound.

Imagine if we shared the wealth, Worked together in good health. But you, dear West, prefer it all, Afraid of Africa standing tall.

The thought of us without your chains, Must surely drive you half-insane. For freedom's sweet, but not for us, Without your grip, it's all a fuss.

You force us to choose your side, Against enemies, real or implied. Yet claim you stand for freedom's call, While building yet another wall.

Democracy, your sacred song, But only when it strings along. For when we exercise our right, Freedom suddenly takes flight.

Oh, what irony, what grand display, Freedom's only true your way. For when an African stands free, It's unacceptable, you see.

Our vast resources, shared and fair, Would leave more wealth beyond compare. But no, you hoard, you clutch, you cling, To every diamond, every ring.

Perhaps you worry, in the end, Of a world where we don't depend. A world where Africa can rise, Without your boots, without your ties.

So here's to you, the Western might, Who preaches freedom, keeps it tight. The irony, so clear, so bright, As Africa remains in night.

But one day soon, we'll find our way, And on that bright, unfettered day, We'll share our riches, true and fair, And show the world how much we care.

For freedom's more than just a word, It's a right that will be heard. And in that future, bold and bright, We'll stand together, free in light.

Oh, hail the West with noble hand

Oh, hail the West with noble hand, Bestowers of aid on African land. With smiles so wide and pockets deep, They sow the seeds that make us weep.

Bilateral and multilateral aid, With promises so grandly made. They claim to help, to lift, to grow, But what they reap, we surely know.

Their coffers full, they hand us loans, In currency that chills our bones. The interest high, the terms unfair, A cunning trap, a debt to bear.

They speak of growth, of futures bright, Yet keep us bound in endless night. For every dollar that they give, Our hopes diminish, dreams relive.

Dependency, their hidden goal, To keep us in a beggar's role. Our leaders bow, their hands outstretched, Their power, our progress, deeply etched.

With aid comes strings, a puppet's thread, They pull, we dance, our spirits bled. Economic plans, they dictate so, Organic growth, we'll never know.

They strip our resources, fuel their might, Then toss us crumbs, to quell the fight. Our industries, they stifle, crush, While in our ears, their praises gush.

Infrastructure built on shaky ground, A gift, they say, but we're bound. To systems weak, to plans unmade, By every dollar of their aid.

The West's a friend, or so they claim, Yet keep us poor, in hunger's name. For as we toil and as we strive, They ensure we'll never thrive.

So hail the aid, the grand facade, A masquerade, a cruel charade. For in their wealth, our chains are cast, To keep us mired in the past.

But one day soon, we'll rise and see, The truth behind their charity. And break the chains, and stand alone, With growth organic, strength our own.

For Africa's spirit, wild and free, Will one day claim its destiny. And to the West, we'll send our thanks, For teaching us to break their ranks.

Oh, sing the tales of distant lands

Oh, sing the tales of distant lands, Where Western and Arab hands, With crosses high and crescents bright, Brought Africa to darkest night.

They came with ships, with chains and might, Took our best, our future bright. From villages and fields so green, To distant shores where pain was seen.

Forced labor was the grand design, To build their wealth, our lives malign. Our strongest sons, our daughters fair, Were sold like beasts, with hearts laid bare.

Then back they came with flags unfurled, To colonize this fractured world. The remnants left, with hope so thin, Were ruled again by foreign kin.

Independence, they did bestow, An empty flag, a grand faux show. With borders drawn by hands so cold, Creating conflicts, ages old.

They sliced the land, they split the tribes, With pens and maps, and dark asides. And laughed as brothers turned to foes, In conflicts where the blood still flows.

Visas now, their walls so high, They watch us struggle, sigh, and cry. We're closed out from their golden lands, Controlled by Bretton Woods' demands.

The institutions, firm and strong, Dictate to us where we belong. Economies, they shape and bend, To keep us poor, our spirits penned.

Oh, Christian lands and Arab might, In history's shadows, out of sight. They built their empires on our backs, Then watched as progress slowly cracks.

With prayers and books, they came to save, But led us to an endless grave. Our wealth and strength, they took away, Then left us in this disarray.

Oh, what grand tales the history writes, Of Western and Arabian plights. A legacy of blood and tears, That's lasted through these countless years.

But still, beneath the weight we bear, Africa rises, unaware. For in our hearts, the spirit lives, A strength that nothing ever gives.

And someday soon, the world will see, An Africa, proud and free. With borders mended, hearts aligned, A future bright, our past behind.

So here's to them, the hypocrites, Whose legacy is built on bits, Of broken lives and shattered dreams, But Africa will rise, it seems.

Every Life Matters: A Sarcastic Refrain

Every life matters, or so they say, But in Africa, it feels a different way. The UN, with its grand decrees, Do they see our lives beneath the trees?

"Every life matters," a noble creed, Yet when we bleed, who takes the lead? The UK-based Commonwealth, so proud, But do they hear us cry aloud?

The World Trade Organization, grand, With policies that squeeze our land. IMF, with its strings so tight, Does every African life hold light?

Pharmaceutical giants, bold and true, In the COVID wake, what did they do? Vaccines promised, vaccines sold, Yet millions left out in the cold.

"Every life matters," the banner waves, But who steps in when the digging graves? A slogan bright, a shining dream, But in Africa, it's a silent scream.

The UN's meetings, grand and long, With speeches, votes, and righteous song. Yet on the ground, where is the care? Do they even know we're there?

The Commonwealth, a brotherhood, Bound by history, so they stood. But when we falter, when we fall, Do they really hear our call?

World Trade talks, so fair, so just, Yet in their wake, our dreams are dust. Economic growth, they say, is near, But for us, it's loss and fear.

IMF, with loans so vast, Promises a future fast. Yet debts grow tall, and hope grows thin, Do they see the state we're in?

Big Pharma, with their global reach, Preaches care, but what's the breach? COVID struck, and profits soared, While Africa's needs were ignored.

"Every life matters," they proclaim, Yet here, it feels a hollow name. A chant that rings in distant lands, While Africa struggles, and no one stands.

So here's to every life that's dear, A truth that seems so insincere. For when the world declares its care, We look around and see the air.

Every life matters, a call so grand, But does it hold in Africa's land? A dream we chase, a hope we cling, In a world that barely hears a thing.

Oh, hail the leaders

Oh, hail the leaders, once so grand, Who claimed to free our cherished land. With speeches bold, they took the stage, A new dawn promised, a golden age.

But lo and behold, the tale's retold, As they, too, sought the power and gold. From colonial chains, we thought we'd fly, Only to see new tyrants nigh.

They wear the flags, they don the pride, But in their hearts, the truth they hide. They oppress us like we're an offence, Their rule, a sham, a grand pretence.

They bow and scrape to foreign thrones, While making us feel like foreign clones. Our land, once ours, now seems so strange, As they, the bootlickers, rearrange.

The coups, they come with thunderous might, Promising to set things right. But each new ruler, in turn, betrays, And leads us through the same old maze.

A vicious circle, coup de tat, Where hope is crushed by those who spat. On dreams of freedom, justice, peace, Instead, our woes, they do increase.

Our leaders dance to foreign tunes, Beneath the sun, beneath the moons. Their masters smile, their pockets swell, While we remain in this living hell.

They build their mansions, high and grand, While hunger grips our barren land. Our voices silenced, dreams denied, In our own home, we're cast aside.

Oh, independence, what a ruse, A tragic tale we didn't choose. From colonizers' grasp, we thought we'd flee, But now we serve new tyranny.

The promises, so bright, so bold, Now lay in ruins, growing cold. For every leader who took the helm, Turned our land into their realm.

But still, we hope, and still, we dream, That one day soon, a true regime, Will rise and lift our spirits high, Beneath a free and open sky.

So here's to them, the leaders grand, Who turned our dreams to dust and sand. The former, neo-colonialists in disguise, But Africa's spirit will one day rise.

Oh the Pearl!

Oh, how grand the Pearl of Africa glows, With riches reaped from where nobody knows. A leader so wise, so just, so pure, Drives a fleet of cars while the people endure.

To Bretton Woods he sends his plea, For borrowed money, not for you or me, But for his kin, his cronies, his band, Living in luxury across this blessed land.

The future's burden? Why should he care? Posterity's plight is not his to bear. In villages where hunger bites and gnaws, He zips by in splendor, without a pause.

A Pan African, he proudly proclaims, While his people toil in poverty's flames. Mismanagement? No, it's a masterful plan, To fatten the pockets of this noble man.

Oh, what a leader, what a shining star, Guiding his nation from the backseat of a car. The Pearl of Africa, so rich, so grand, Mismanaged to perfection by his steady hand.

The Glowing Riches of the Pearl

Oh, how grand the Pearl of Africa glows, With riches reaped from where nobody knows. Beneath the fertile soil and lush landscapes, Lie resources untapped, wealth that escapes.

Gold, diamonds, and oil, hidden from sight, Promising prosperity, a future so bright. Yet, mysteriously, these riches don't flow, To the common folk, their struggles still grow.

The Wise Leader's Splendor

A leader so wise, so just, so pure, Drives a fleet of cars while the people endure. With pomp and pageantry, he parades around, In luxury vehicles, his greatness is crowned.

While children go hungry, and mothers weep, He navigates roads in cars sleek and steep. His palace shines bright with opulence and grace, An ironic beacon in a suffering place.

The Plea to Bretton Woods

To Bretton Woods he sends his plea, For borrowed money, not for you or me, But for his kin, his cronies, his band, Living in luxury across this blessed land.

Loans and aid, the lifeblood of his reign, Secured with promises that never sustain. Infrastructure projects that never quite start, Funds diverted with a sleight of hand art.

The Burden of the Future

The future's burden? Why should he care? Posterity's plight is not his to bear. The weight of debt, a chain for tomorrow, For the leader, a distant, detached sorrow.

In villages where hunger bites and gnaws, He zips by in splendor, without a pause. The cries of the needy, a background noise, Drowned by the hum of his luxurious toys.

The Pan African Proclamation

A Pan African, he proudly proclaims, While his people toil in poverty's flames. Uniting a continent with speeches grand, But failing his nation, unable to withstand.

Mismanagement? No, it's a masterful plan, To fatten the pockets of this noble man. Strategic incompetence, a ruse so deft, Ensuring his wealth while little is left.

The Shining Star Leader

Oh, what a leader, what a shining star, Guiding his nation from the backseat of a car. The roads he travels, smooth and wide, A stark contrast to paths where commoners stride.

The Pearl of Africa, so rich, so grand, Mismanaged to perfection by his steady hand. A tale of wealth hoarded, dreams deferred, Of a nation's potential, forever blurred.

The Illusion of Progress

Progress, he claims, in speeches and reports, Echoed by ministers and supportive cohorts. Yet, beneath the surface, the truth is clear, Stagnation and decay, year after year.

Development projects announced with flair, But tangible results are exceedingly rare. Schools, hospitals, roads left in decay, While funds intended simply fade away.

The People's Resilience

Amidst the grandeur, the people persist, With resilience and hope, they continue to exist. Farmers till fields with tools old and worn, Merchants trade goods from dawn until morn.

Communities bind together, strong and tight, Facing hardships with collective might. In the face of neglect, they forge ahead, Determined to survive, even as they're misled.

The Legacy of the Pearl

The legacy of the Pearl, complex and vast, A testament to potential squandered fast. A nation rich in resources and heart, Held back by leadership that plays the wrong part.

Oh, Pearl of Africa, so rich, so grand, May one day your people truly understand, That true prosperity lies not in gold or decree, But in fair governance and true equity.

A Hope for Change

Yet, hope lingers in the hearts of the young, A vision of change, a new song to be sung. Dreams of leaders who truly will care, To lift the burden, to play fair.

Oh, the Pearl! May you one day shine, With justice, prosperity, and progress aligned. May your leaders serve with integrity clear, And bring forth the future your people hold dear.

The exploiter

In the heart of the bustling city, where hope is as scarce as rain in a drought, there stands a towering church beside a grand government building. Both promise salvation, both promise change, but their methods, oh, how they differ in name alone.

The church, with its high steeples and resounding bells, collects its dues under the guise of tithes and offerings. "Give, and you shall receive," they preach, their coffers swelling with the hard-earned coins of the poor. The congregation, seeking solace and salvation, part with their meager earnings, dreaming of a heavenly mansion promised in the hereafter.

Across the street, the government demands its share, cloaked in the authority of taxes and levies. "For the good of the nation," they declare, as they siphon away the sweat of the people's brow. The citizens, burdened with heavy hearts and light wallets, comply in the hope of better roads, schools, and hospitals, which remain perpetually under construction.

The irony is palpable. In the church, the preacher dons a robe of silk, feasting on the finest wines and meats, while his flock goes hungry, assured that their reward awaits in the afterlife. In the government halls, the officials drive luxury cars and reside in palatial homes, all while their constituents wait in long lines for a drop of clean water and a glimpse of a doctor.

The promises echo, both divine and secular: "Your sacrifice will be rewarded." Yet, the rewards are reserved for the elite, the shepherds of faith and the stewards of the state, who share a common trait—the ability to spin gold from the gullibility of the masses.

And so, the poor give and give, in church pews and tax offices, expecting celestial riches or infrastructural miracles. But in the end, they find themselves stuck in the same cycle of poverty, their sacrifices funding the luxurious lives of those they trust.

The difference between the church and the government? Merely the nomenclature of their collections. The result? The same—an ever-widening gap between the haves and the have-nots, with the former basking in the luxuries of this life, while promising the latter a better existence, either in the next world or in a perpetually elusive future.

Oh, hail the international band

Oh, hail the international band, Who watched as Rwanda's fate was planned. In '94, they turned away, Pretending they had naught to say.

The West, with all its might and grace, Ignored the cries, the terror's face. "No strategic interest here," They said, and brushed away the fear.

A genocide, a blood-soaked land, While they discussed with wringing hands. "No interference," came the call, As bodies piled and cities fall.

The looters, with their greedy eyes, Kept silent as they watched the cries. A blind eye turned, a deaf ear lent, While all their hollow words were spent.

"Local affairs," they claimed, so pure, And watched as death walked through the door. No oil, no gold, no precious stake, So why, for Rwanda, should they wake?

The UN spoke with earnest tones, But left the Rwandans on their own. A peacekeeping force, so small, so weak, Became a tragic, sad critique.

The nations sat in grand debate, While genocide became the fate. For every life that's lost, they're cursed, By hands that should have stopped the worst.

"Never again," they'd proudly cried, But when it came, they stepped aside. The horrors bloomed, the blood did flow, And all the world had watched the show.

Oh, international community, Your apathy, a true calamity. For in those days of darkest plight, You chose to turn away from sight.

So here's to you, the great and just, Who let Rwanda turn to dust. Your noble stance, your hands so clean, A darkened blotch on history's screen.

But let this be a bitter tale, Of how humanity can fail. For while they spoke of peace and care, They left Rwanda in despair.

And in the hearts of those who bled, A memory of the words unsaid. The world's neglect, a silent scream, A haunting, never-ending dream.

Behold the king

Behold the king of grand charades, A president, in bright parades. With smiles and suits, he takes the stage, A puppet in a gilded cage.

His people's cries are but a hum, A background noise, a bothersome. Why care for those who till the land, When foreign praise is close at hand?

He struts and preens for foreign eyes, In their approval, his heart lies. Their handshakes and their shallow praise, Outshine his people's tear-streaked gaze.

For them, he bends, he bows, he kneels, Their interests are the truest deals. His coffers swell with foreign gold, While stories of his wealth are told.

At home, his whip cracks sharp and loud, To silence any rising crowd. Dissent is crushed beneath his boot, He reigns with fear, his power absolute.

The schools decay, the clinics rot, But he, in mansions, cares not a jot. The markets empty, bellies bare, While he enjoys his banquet fare.

He flies in jets to lands afar, While roads at home remain bizarre. With every trip, his pockets grow, As poverty remains below.

His speeches, oh so grand, so grand, In foreign tongues, on distant land. He boasts of progress, peace, and growth, While truth lies murdered by his oath.

But hush, dear people, do not speak, Your voices weak, your future bleak. For he's a star on foreign stage, Your woes are but an empty page.

To him, your lives are cheap and small, In his grand play, you matter not at all. His kingdom built on lies and gold, A legacy of truth untold.

So bow, oh masses, to your king, For he has wealth and foreign bling. Your hopes, your dreams, they mean so little, In his grand game, you're just a riddle.

And as he smiles, his pockets filled, Remember how your cries were stilled. A president, a tyrant, a clown, Who wears deceit as his true crown.

Behold the lord of grand pretence

Behold the lord of grand pretence, A president of no defence. With empty words and grand display, He rules the land in disarray.

Nepotism is his creed, His family's greed a growing weed. His wife, a minister, so grand, While children hold the nation's hand.

A brother here, a sister there, They grasp the purse, they take their share. In lavish homes they sit and feast, While common folk survive the least.

The hospitals, they cry for aid, But infants die, the bills unpaid. He lifts his hands in public prayer, Pretending that he's truly there.

The national prayer breakfast scene, Where piety is worn so clean. He sounds the drums of holy might, While turning from the public plight.

He loves the red carpet's plush embrace, The flash of cameras on his face. His speeches blast colonial sins, While deep corruption wins and wins.

Patriotic songs, he loudly sings, Of freedom's joy and hopeful springs. Yet worse than traders of the past, His grip on power holds us fast.

He mocks the chains of history, While forging new ones, can't you see? For in his reign, the people fall, Their cries unheard beyond his wall.

A puppet king, a grand charade, With every move, our hopes betrayed. He preaches love for native land, Yet robs us blind with every hand.

So here's to him, the mighty fool, Who thinks he's clever, thinks he'll rule. But history sees and history knows, The hollow man, in emperor's clothes.

And as he dances on the stage, Our anger builds, our hearts enraged. For we, the people, will arise, To cast away his throne of lies.

For now, we watch the tragic play, The farce that leads our lives astray. A president of pomp and show, Whose legacy is naught but woe.

Behold the mighty parliament

Behold the mighty parliament, A circus show of grand intent. Where words are tossed in empty air, And promises dissolve to nowhere.

Our parliamentarian stands so proud, Amidst the laughter of the crowd. He speaks of justice, peace, and right, While darkness falls on every light.

He struts and preens in tailored suits, A puppet with no real pursuits. His pockets lined with bribes and gold, His conscience lost, his morals sold.

In Uganda's halls, they take their stand, A rubberstamp for the king's command. They nod and cheer, they raise their hands, To loot the wealth, to rob the lands.

United in their grand charade, They split the spoils, a slick brigade. When it's time to steal and scheme, They move as one, a perfect team.

But ask them for the people's care, And watch them falter, duck, and stare. On matters that the masses need, They're ever doggy, slow to heed.

The people's cries, they do not hear, Their hopes and dreams are nowhere near. They vote for laws that fill their purse, While life for us keeps getting worse.

In hallowed halls, they take their seat, In leather chairs, with snacks to eat. Debates that drone, that go nowhere, While hunger's grip is everywhere.

His speeches crafted, oh so fine, With rhetoric, he draws the line. He blames the past, he blames the West, But never turns to face the mess.

The parliament, a grand charade, Where deals are made, and truths betrayed. They clap and cheer, they raise a toast, To all the things that matter most.

But where are roads, where is the aid? Where is the progress that they made? In villages, the children cry, While parliamentarians lie.

The hospitals, the schools, the streets, Are crumbling beneath their feet. Yet in their world of endless perks, They're blind to how their system works.

The parliamentarian grins and waves, Oblivious to the lives he saves. For in his world of pomp and flair, The people's pain is but thin air.

So let us watch this tragic play, The parliament in grand display. A farce, a joke, a sad parade, Of promises and deals betrayed.

For one day soon, the tide will turn, The fires of change will fiercely burn. And those who've mocked our desperate pleas, Will face the wrath of rising seas.

Behold the hallowed halls of law

Behold the hallowed halls of law, The judiciary, without a flaw. Or so they claim, with robes and stance, A tragic farce, a hollow dance.

The temple of justice, once so grand, Now crumbles beneath a corrupt hand. For in these courts, where truth should reign, Deceit and greed have left a stain.

The mighty judges, in their gowns, Wear solemn faces, hide their frowns. Behind the bench, where they preside, Lies influence they cannot hide.

The bureaucrats with power vast, Have seized the courtrooms, held them fast. They peddle influence, bribe and sway, And justice slowly fades away.

The scales of justice, tipped and torn, By golden coins and secret scorn. The law is sold to highest bid, Where truth and fairness now lie hid.

A whisper here, a nod, a wink, And justice teeters on the brink. For those with power, wealth, and might, Can bend the law, can twist the right.

The common folk, they come in hope, But find the courthouse just a trope. Their pleas unheard, their cries ignored, As justice bows to power's sword.

The judges, once with hearts of steel, Now dance to tunes that powers deal. Their gavels fall on hollow ground, Where truth and fairness can't be found.

In chambers dark, where deals are made, The righteous path begins to fade. For every bribe, for every lie, Another piece of justice dies.

So let us watch this tragic play, The judiciary in disarray. A stage where actors feign and preen, In robes that once were pure and clean.

But soon the people's voice will rise, And sweep away the web of lies. For justice, though now bruised and bent, Will find its way, its true ascent.

And those who've stained this sacred hall, Will face the reckoning of all. For in the end, truth's light will shine, And cleanse the courts of their decline.

Behold the grand cathedral's might

Behold the grand cathedral's might, Once a beacon in the night. Mainstream churches, proud and tall, Now bow to cash, they heed the call.

Their mission once was pure and true, To denounce the wrong, uphold the few. Prophetic voices rang so clear, But now they're lost, we hardly hear.

The pastors, priests, in robes adorned, Have traded truth for wealth unearned. A hand of cash, a brown envelope, Has turned their message into smoke.

The mighty wield illegitimate power, And churches bend, they cringe, they cower. No longer do they speak for right, But blind the masses with false light.

The pulpit once a place of fire, Now serves the whims of those much higher. Their sermons filled with hollow praise, For tyrants in their gilded maze.

Gone are the days of righteous cries, Replaced by silence, coated lies. The church, a voice of subjugation, Betrays the masses, seeds frustration.

The poor, the weak, who seek relief, Find only pretence, veiled in grief. For in the halls where hymns should rise, Now echo greed and compromise.

The pastors preach prosperity, While turning blind to poverty. Their prayers for peace, a grand charade, As suffering people feel betrayed.

The hands that bless, the hands that take, Are stained with gold for heaven's sake. The shepherds lead their flocks astray, With promises that fade away.

And as the rich grow ever bold, The church's silence, bought and sold. No longer do they challenge sin, For fear of losing what they win.

Yet in the hearts of those who yearn, The fire of truth will always burn. And someday soon, the church will face, The reckoning of its disgrace.

For faith is not a thing to trade, Nor truth a game that can be played. The prophets' call, though silenced now, Will rise again, reclaim the vow.

So let us watch this tragic play, The mainstream church in disarray. A farce of faith, a grand betrayal, But truth and justice will prevail.

Ah, the Social Contract

Ah, the Social Contract, what a splendid myth! That quaint little idea that power belongs to the people, a fairy tale whispered in the corridors of history and political theory. Let's take a moment to marvel at this grand illusion, shall we?

Once upon a time, the noble concept of the Social Contract was born, promising that the rulers would govern with the consent of the governed. Power to the people, they proclaimed! What a joke. As if the people ever really had a say. The masses, in their infinite wisdom, were told that their votes and voices mattered, that they could shape the destiny of their nation. And oh, how they believed it!

In the grand halls of government, those elected to serve the people—oh, what a term of endearment—sit upon their thrones, sipping the finest wines and feasting on gourmet meals, all while drafting policies that are as beneficial to the common folk as a plague. They pontificate about liberty and justice, all the while ensuring that their pockets are lined and their power is unchallenged.

The people, bless their hearts, gather in the town squares, waving their banners and chanting their slogans, convinced that their voices will be heard. They march for change, they vote for hope, and they pray for a better tomorrow. Meanwhile, the leaders chuckle behind closed doors, knowing full well that the system is rigged, the game is fixed, and the people's role is merely to provide the illusion of democracy.

"Power belongs to the people," they say, as they sign off on laws that strip away freedoms, impose new taxes, and funnel wealth upwards. The people's power, it seems, is limited to choosing which puppet will dance for them on the political stage, while the real strings are pulled by the unseen hands of the elite.

Every election cycle, the people are given the grand choice between the lesser of two evils, a selection as meaningful as picking the color of their chains. They vote, they hope, and then they wait, as the promises of change evaporate like morning dew, leaving behind the same old status quo.

And so, the Social Contract remains an eternal failure, a joke played on the gullible masses. The power, it turns out, never belonged to the people. It was always an elaborate ruse, a comforting lie to keep them docile and compliant. The leaders rule, the people obey, and the cycle continues, a testament to the enduring absurdity of believing that the many could ever truly hold sway over the few.

Oh, the United Nations!

Oh, the United Nations! What a marvelous assembly of nations, a beacon of hope for global unity, equality, and sovereignty. Let's all take a moment to admire this grand theater of international diplomacy.

Imagine the scene: delegates from every corner of the globe, dressed in their finest, gathering to discuss and resolve the world's most pressing issues. Each nation, regardless of size or power, has an equal voice, they claim. Equality of nations, they proclaim! What a splendid fantasy. As if the voices of the powerful weren't drowning out the rest.

In theory, sovereignty is sacrosanct. Each nation is free to govern itself without interference. But let's not kid ourselves. The reality? A grand show where the strong dictate terms and the weak nod along, hoping for scraps from the table. Sovereignty, it seems, is just a fancy word for "do as we say or face the consequences."

Then there's the unipolar world, dominated by a single superpower that calls the shots, ensuring its interests are protected under the guise of promoting global stability. The United Nations, in this context, becomes a tool, a stage for the powerful to flex their muscles while pretending to care about international law and justice. Resolutions are passed, vetoes are cast, and the illusion of consensus is maintained. But everyone knows who's really in charge.

Oh, but wait! There's the noble struggle for multipolarity, the valiant effort by emerging powers to create a balanced world order where no single nation can dominate. How quaint. The idea that multiple power centers can coexist and collaborate equally is as believable as a fairy tale. The reality is a constant tug-of-war, a game of geopolitical chess where the rules are written by the winners.

Equality of nations? Only if you believe that a lion and a lamb have equal chances in a cage match. Sovereignty? As long as it doesn't conflict with the interests of the big players. Multipolarity? A dream for those tired of the unipolar world's heavy hand, but still a distant mirage.

And for Africa? We're like mere observers in this grand spectacle. Our leaders, bless their hearts, resemble school prefects whose speeches are but a ritual signifying nothing. They stand at the podium, deliver their well-rehearsed lines about unity and progress, and then return to their seats, having achieved little more than participating in a charade. They play their part, not to effect real change, but to keep up appearances in a game rigged against them from the start.

So, here we are, applauding the grand performance of the United Nations, pretending that it's anything more than a stage for power politics. The eternal failure of these lofty ideals is as predictable as the rising sun. The strong rule, the weak follow, and the struggle for a truly equal and sovereign world continues to be a grand illusion, a comforting lie told to those who still believe in fairy tales.

There rose a man shrouded

In the heart of the Congo, where rivers pulse through emerald veins and jungles whisper ancient secrets, there rose a man shrouded in dread and enigma.

His name was Muramba, a name that echoed through the valleys and villages with the weight of fear and reverence.

He was no ordinary warlord, but a spectre of cruelty, draped in the tattered robes of divinity.Muramba believed himself chosen, his every action sanctified by a voice that only he could hear.

In the quiet of the night, when the moon cast silver threads upon the dense canopy, he would stand alone, eyes closed, lips moving in silent prayer to the gods he claimed to serve.

These gods were dark and vengeful, demanding blood and suffering as their homage.

He led his men with a zealot's fervour, their loyalty bound by a shared myth of celestial endorsement.They swept through villages like a storm, leaving a trail of ashes and despair.

Houses burned, and the night skies were painted with the crimson hue of sorrow. The cries of the innocent mingled with the howls of the night creatures, creating a symphony of agony that reverberated through the land.

Muramba's exploits were grotesque, tales told in hushed tones around dying fires. He wielded power with a hand of iron and a heart of ice, believing each atrocity a necessary rite, each slaughter a sacred sacrifice. He fashioned himself a prophet of doom, his eyes gleaming with the fire of his self-righteous cause.

His men followed blindly, seeing in his madness a twisted form of salvation, a promise of glory amidst the ruins.

Yet, in the shadows of his mind, doubt lurked. In the silent moments between battles, he would question the voice, the divine call that had set him on this path of ruin. But these moments were fleeting, swallowed by the abyss of his convictions.

He clung to his belief as a drowning man clings to driftwood, fearing the abyss of his own insignificance more than the blood that stained his hands.

The land groaned under the weight of his tyranny, the forests and rivers bearing silent witness to the unfolding nightmare.

Legends grew around his figure, stories of a man who had bargained with gods for power, who had traded his soul for the ability to command life and death.

Children learned to fear his name, mothers wept for their lost sons, and the elders prayed for deliverance from the madness that had taken root in their world.But in the end, all tyrants face their reckoning.

Muramba's came not with the clamour of battle but in the quiet of the dawn.

Alone, atop a hill overlooking the land he had ravaged, he stood as the first light of day broke through the horizon.

The voice that had guided him was silent, the gods he had served absent. In that moment, he was just a man, stripped of his divine pretence, facing the enormity of his sins.

As the sun rose, casting its golden glow over the Congo, the warlord known as Muramba fell to his knees, his tears mingling with the dew.

The earth, once stained with the blood of his conquests, seemed to breathe a sigh of relief.

And in that fragile light of morning, the jungle began to heal, reclaiming its ancient rhythm, whispering once more of secrets and dreams, and the dark legend of Muramba faded into the annals of forgotten nightmares.

In the heart of Africa

In the heart of Africa, where the sun bleeds red, A child's eyes mirror the pain where hope has fled.

Tiny hands clutch dreams, now tattered and torn, In a land where innocence is prematurely worn.

War drums beat, a cruel symphony of despair, While modern warlords, with gilded tongues, declare Themselves as saviours, champions of the land, Yet with blood-stained fingers, they carve their stand.

Amongst the ruins where laughter once grew, An African child, with eyes of deep, endless blue, Wanders through the remnants of a shattered life, Where the promise of peace is silenced by strife.

The liberators dine on gold and deceit, Their lavish banquets blind to the child in the street.

They speak of freedom, of futures bright and clear, Yet their promises drown in rivers of fear.Beneath the shadows of war's cruel embrace, A child searches for a lost, familiar face.

Innocence lost, traded for tears and sorrow, Dreams postponed, yearning for a brighter tomorrow.

Oh, African child, your silent cries resound, Through the heart of the world, a haunting sound.

May your pain be the seed of a future reborn, Where peace, not war, is the legacy worn.

For within your suffering, a strength is forged anew, A testament to the spirit that dwells within you.

May the world awaken to the truth in your eyes, And rise against the warlords' deceitful lies.

In lands where sun and shadow blend

In lands where sun and shadow blend, Where hope and hardship never end, The tale of health care we unfold, A story often left untold. No insurance, no safety net, For many dreams are unmet. State support, a distant dream, In this relentless, harsh regime.

Babies born in humble homes, No sterile wards, no cushioned domes. No soft bed for mother's rest, Just earth and grit, a daunting test.

Herbs and roots, our ancient lore, The healers' hands we can't ignore. For in the absence of the new, The old ways guide us through and through.

The clinics, few and far between, With weary walls and air unseen. Doctors scarce, their faces drawn, By endless battles, night till dawn.

Medicines, a rare delight, Too often, they're just out of sight. Yet through the pain, the fear, the strife, We find a way to cling to life.

In villages, where strength is born, We rise with every breaking morn. Resilient hearts, enduring souls, We press ahead, despite the tolls.

Mothers cradle newborns tight, Their lullabies a soft, brave light. In fields and huts, beneath the skies, Their songs of hope refuse to die.

No shiny hospitals in sight, But still we fight, with all our might. For in the face of great despair, We find the will to deeply care.

Our health care, fragile, under strain, Yet through it all, we bear the pain. With spirits strong and hearts so vast, We forge ahead, outlasting past.

For every child, for every breath, We challenge fate, we battle death. And though the road is rough and long, We journey on, enduring strong.

In lands where sun and shadow blend, Our story's one that will not end. Through herbs and hands, through ancient lore, We heal, we hope, we strive for more.

The Untold reality of an African Girl

In a village cloaked in night's silent song, A girl was born where hope seemed gone. Beneath the sun's relentless blaze, She wandered through her childhood's haze.

Her name was whispered on the wind, A symbol of dreams that once had been. Her eyes, a mirror of the sky, Reflected dreams now left to die.

In fields where gold should kiss the earth, She toiled for every grain's worth. The land, so rich, yet pockets bare, Her family trapped in stark despair.

The rivers flowed with wealth unseen, While she fetched water from a stream. Beneath her feet, the diamonds lay, Yet hunger marked her every day.

The nationalists, in suits of lies, Promised lands of azure skies. They came with flags, with drums, with cheers, And left with coffers filled for years.

In shadows deep, the deals were made, The multinationals' greed displayed. They siphoned riches, unseen by eyes, And left behind the girl's soft cries. Her school a hut, her books a dream, Her future lost in silent screams. For every coin, her laughter sold, Her story left, so often, untold.

Yet in her heart, a fire burned, A yearning for a life unearned. She dreamed of days where she could soar, Beyond the village, to distant shores.

Beneath the weight of skies so blue, She grew in strength, her spirit true. For though the darkness veiled her light, She held on tight, through endless night.

Her voice, a whisper in the wind, A tale of strength that would not bend. And in her song, a truth profound, Of stolen wealth, of hopes unbound.

In every village girl's soft sigh, A call for justice in the sky. For though the riches leave in haste, Their spirits rise, no more erased.

The untold reality of an African boy

In the heart of an African dawn, A boy was born where hope seemed gone. Beneath the sky so vast and wide, He learned to live, he learned to hide.

His name was whispered with the breeze, A symbol of forgotten pleas. His eyes, a mirror of the night, Held dreams that struggled for the light.

In lands of green where riches gleamed, He worked for scraps, for distant dreams. The soil, so rich with hidden gold, Yet poverty's grip was tight and cold.The rivers sang of wealth untold, While he fetched water, growing old. Beneath his feet, the treasures lay, But hunger shadowed every day.

The nationalists, in robes of pride, Promised a future, far and wide. They spoke of freedom, of days anew, And left with wealth that grew and grew.

In secret rooms, the pacts were signed, The multinationals' greed aligned. They took the diamonds, the oil, the land, And left the boy with empty hands.

His school, a dream, a distant place, His life, a never-ending race. For every coin, a piece of soul, His future buried in a hole.

Yet in his heart, a flame burned bright, A yearning for a better sight. He dreamed of days where he could rise, Beyond the lies, beyond the skies.

Beneath the weight of endless toil, He stood his ground, on native soil. For though the world had turned away, He fought to see a brighter day.

His voice, a murmur in the night, A story of unyielding fight. And in his song, a truth revealed, Of stolen dreams, of wounds unhealed.

In every village boy's clear eyes, A call for justice never dies. For though the riches fade from sight, Their spirits soar, in endless flight.

A toiling mother in Africa

In the heart of Africa's embrace, A mother's journey, quiet grace. Her tale untold, her struggles deep, In shadows where the silence creeps.

Beneath the sun's relentless glare, She walks with burdens hard to bear. Her strength, a river flowing strong, In lands where right is often wrong.

Her belly swells with life anew, Yet care and aid are far and few. The clinics bare, the doctors gone, Her battles fought from dusk to dawn.

With each new day, her steps grow slow, Her weary eyes with pain do glow. In fields she labors, bends, and kneels, Her cries absorbed by silent hills.

Her nights are long, the darkness cold, Her dreams of help, of hands to hold. But promises are empty shells, Left by leaders with empty wells.

The nationalists, in mansions grand, Forget the mother's calloused hand. Their coffers filled with ill-gained gold, While she, in dust, remains unsold.

The multinationals, with greedy eyes, Strip the land and weave their lies. They leave behind a barren trace, A mother's tears on a weathered face.

Yet in her heart, a fire burns, A fierce resolve that never turns. For every life she brings to light, She wages war with all her might.

In lullabies she softly sings, Of hope and dreams, of better things. Her voice, a beacon in the dark, Ignites the night with a tiny spark.

Her story, whispered by the breeze, Is one of strength that never flees. A testament to all she bears, A call for justice, unawares.

For every mother's silent cry, Is written in the endless sky. And though her struggles seem concealed, Her spirit's truth will be revealed.

In every child's bright, hopeful eyes, A glimpse of her undying ties. For though the world may turn away, Her legacy will find its way.

A Woman in Africa

In a land where shadows cast long shades, A woman's tale in silence fades. Her children's cries, a mournful song, In a world where right is often wrong.

Her sons are taken, bound to fight, For warlords' gain, for darkened might. Like slaves they toil, their youth consumed, In fields where innocence is entombed.

Her daughters too, in silence weep, Their dreams sold cheap, their hopes to keep. In homes where darkness shrouds the day, Their laughter lost, their light betrayed.

She works from dawn to setting sun, Her battle never truly won. In poverty, she raises high, Her children's dreams beneath the sky.

The government, a distant ghost, Appears when they can take the most. They fleece her of her meager gains, Her hard-earned coins in coffers' chains.

Where is the conscience, where's the heart, Of those who play the noble part? The elite, the moral, Jack and Jane, Who watch and yet ignore the pain.

In halls of power, in rooms of light, They turn away from sorrow's sight. Their speeches grand, their actions few, Her plight unseen, her suffering true.

Yet still she stands, with weary grace, A warrior in life's harsh embrace. Her love a shield, her hope a flame, That burns despite the endless shame.

Her eyes, though tired, reflect the sky, A testament that will not die. For though the world may turn away, Her spirit fights another day.

Her children's dreams, her silent plea, A call for justice, to be free. In every tear, a story told, Of strength and love, of hearts so bold.

And someday, when the world awakes, When conscience stirs and justice shakes, Her tale will rise, her truth will shine, A beacon bright, a sacred sign.

For in her struggle, in her fight, She holds the dawn, she births the light. A mother's love, a force unseen, The truest power ever been.

Oh, the rich tapestry of global diplomacy!

Oh, the rich tapestry of global diplomacy! World leaders, ever the paragons of virtue, love to wax poetic about human rights in Africa.

Their heartfelt speeches and stern condemnations truly tug at the heartstrings. It's almost as if they have no idea their own policies and economic interests might just be contributing to the very issues they decry.

But hey, nothing says "we care" like a photo-op with a suffering child and a pledge that will never see the light of day, right?

Bravo, world leaders, for your tireless dedication to appearing morally superior while turning a blind eye to the consequences of your actions.

And let's not forget the pièce de résistance: those sparkling diamonds that enrich your coffers.

Consider every bloody diamond that lines your pockets, and the cries of the simple hands that excavate the hills of Africa for your pleasure. It's truly a testament to your unwavering commitment to human rights. Keep up the good work!

The untold saga of Western hypocrisy

Ah, the untold saga of Western hypocrisy! The narrative is as old as time, yet still as bitter as ever. The aid industry, that ever-so-noble enterprise, keeps churning away, ostensibly to "help" Africa. But scratch the surface, and what do you find? A well-oiled machine designed to keep Africa on its knees, perpetually dependent and shackled by so-called generosity.

Rather than opening their markets to Africa's abundant organic farm and dairy products, Western nations slam the doors shut. The irony is almost poetic. While they preach the gospel of free trade and open markets, they deny Africa the very access that could lead to true economic independence. Instead, they keep the aid flowing, not to uplift, but to maintain the status quo.

And let's talk about where this aid really goes. It's no secret that a significant portion lines the pockets of corrupt African leaders, ensuring that the masses remain in abject poverty. This insidious cycle of dependency and exploitation is a masterclass in maintaining control. Keep the leaders rich, keep the people poor, and keep the resources flowing out.

So here's to the Western world, masters of the double standard. Their aid doesn't free Africa; it chains it. Their trade policies don't empower; they cripple. And all the while, they maintain the façade of benevolence, as if the very system they uphold isn't designed to perpetuate the very problems they claim to solve. Bravo, indeed.

Western treatment of African refugees

Ah, the Western treatment of African refugees fleeing through the Mediterranean—a sterling example of human rights and compassion in action. The lengths to which Western nations go to "protect" and "assist" these desperate souls are nothing short of awe-inspiring. Let's take a closer look at this remarkable display of humanity and respect for human rights.

First, the journey across the Mediterranean is made wonderfully challenging by the Western commitment to rigorous border security. European nations have invested heavily in patrols, barriers, and agreements with North African countries to ensure that refugees have a truly adventurous experience. These measures are designed to teach refugees the value of perseverance and resilience—after all, what doesn't kill you makes you stronger, right?

When refugees do manage to set sail, they are met with the utmost hospitality by Western naval forces. Instead of the simple act of rescue, these forces sometimes opt for the more educational approach of pushing boats back to where they came from, providing refugees with an invaluable lesson in geography and the dangers of unauthorized travel. It's a thoughtful way to ensure that they appreciate the challenges of crossing international waters.

For those who are lucky enough to be rescued, the Western world rolls out the red carpet. They are welcomed into lavishly equipped detention centers, where they can enjoy the finest in minimalist living conditions. These centers, often overcrowded and under-resourced, offer refugees a chance to bond closely with others in similarly dire straits. The lack of basic amenities and healthcare is a subtle encouragement to build a robust immune system and develop a strong sense of community.

Western countries also provide a warm welcome through their immigration policies, which are models of fairness and efficiency. Asylum seekers are treated to lengthy and opaque bureaucratic processes, ensuring that they fully understand the complexities of Western legal systems. This process is designed to be so convoluted that it keeps refugees mentally sharp and constantly engaged, a wonderful exercise in cognitive endurance.

The media portrayal of African refugees is another shining example of Western benevolence. Refugees are often depicted as invaders or economic burdens, a narrative that helps to manage public perception and ensure that local populations remain supportive of stringent immigration policies. This portrayal fosters a sense of unity among Western citizens, as they rally together to protect their borders from the supposed threat of desperate human beings seeking safety.

For those refugees who do manage to secure asylum, the Western nations generously offer them the opportunity to live in marginalized communities, often in squalid conditions. This experience provides refugees with a valuable perspective on the socioeconomic hierarchies and challenges of integration in their new countries. They are also given access to low-wage jobs, which is a wonderful way to introduce them to the joys of capitalism and economic exploitation.

Western governments often collaborate with authoritarian regimes in North Africa to intercept refugees before they even reach the Mediterranean. This partnership ensures that refugees get a taste of the local hospitality in detention camps where their human rights are "respected" in ways that make Western detention centers look like luxury resorts. It's a brilliant example of international cooperation and shared values.

In conclusion, the Western treatment of African refugees fleeing through the Mediterranean is a masterclass in sarcasm. From rigorous border security and hostile naval forces to overcrowded detention centers and dehumanizing media narratives, the West's approach ensures that the human rights of these refugees are "respected" in the most ironic sense possible. It's a testament to the West's commitment to maintaining its image as a bastion of human rights, while simultaneously ensuring that those rights are trampled for the most vulnerable. Truly, a spectacle of modern humanitarianism.

Visa Fees: The Perfect Robbery in Plain Sight

Oh, the grand theater of visa applications—a masterful display of Western benevolence and a testament to the entrepreneurial spirit of modern diplomacy. The Western embassies, those majestic bastions of opportunity and hope, have perfected the art of robbing African youths through the meticulously orchestrated collection of visa fees. It's a marvel of modern-day exploitation, cleverly disguised as border control.

The Art of Stringent Conditions

Let's applaud the Western countries for their creative genius in crafting visa requirements. The list of necessary documents reads like a work of fiction: bank statements, employment letters, property deeds, and more. It's almost as if they're setting a challenge to see who can compile the most absurd collection of paperwork. The best part? Even if the applicants manage to gather all these documents, the outcome is almost preordained—denial. After all, why make the process easy when you can make it a Kafkaesque nightmare?

Embassies: Halls of Opportunity

These embassies, strategically placed in major African cities, are not just buildings; they're symbols of hope, dreams, and, of course, financial exploitation. Every day, lines of young Africans stretch out the door, each person clutching their meticulously prepared applications, each one hoping against hope that they might be the exception. Little do they know, they're walking into a well-oiled machine designed to extract as much money as possible with little intention of granting actual visas.

The Visa Fees Bonanza

Ah, the visa fees—a brilliant scheme. Hundreds of dollars per application, non-refundable of course. It's a fantastic revenue stream! The embassies rake in the cash while providing nothing in return but rejection letters and crushed dreams. It's a win-win for the West: a steady influx of money and a perfectly legal way to say, "Thanks for playing, better luck next time."

The Conjecture of Intent to Stay

And let's not forget the pièce de résistance: the presumption that every African applicant is a potential illegal immigrant. The sheer audacity of rejecting visas based on the conjecture that these young people might remain in the chilly embrace of Western countries is truly remarkable. Never mind their actual intentions or the validity of their reasons for travel. The default assumption is guilt, and the burden of proof lies entirely with the applicant—a rigged game if ever there was one.

The Cold, Hard Rejections

The rejection letters are masterpieces of vague reasoning and bureaucratic jargon. They cite potential overstay risks and insufficient ties to home countries, ignoring the fact that these same countries have been systematically destabilized by the very powers now denying entry. It's a beautifully ironic twist—creating conditions that drive people to seek better lives elsewhere, then slamming the door shut in their faces while pocketing their hard-earned money.

The Enduring Cycle

So, the cycle continues. Young Africans pour their savings into the visa application process, feeding a system designed to extract as much as possible while giving as little as possible in return. The embassies remain open, their coffers full, while the applicants return home empty-handed, having learned a valuable lesson in the economics of exploitation.

In the grand scheme of things, it's a perfect setup. The West maintains its image of opportunity and fairness while quietly reaping the benefits of stringent visa conditions. The embassies stand as monuments to this lucrative practice, a testament to the enduring legacy of economic exploitation. And as long as young Africans continue to dream of a better life abroad, the embassies will remain open, ever ready to collect those precious visa fees.

Let's raise a glass to this marvel of modern diplomacy—a masterclass in exploitation and the ultimate irony of freedom. Cheers to the embassies, the visa fees, and the brilliant scheme that keeps the cycle going strong.

Ah, the Western aid industry

Ah, the Western aid industry—a paragon of altruism and efficiency, where everyone wins, especially the Western powers and Africa's most corrupt leaders. It's a brilliant system that allows Western governments to siphon off taxpayer money under the noble guise of aiding Africa, while ensuring that this aid never quite reaches those in need. Let's delve into this marvel of modern philanthropy and its many layers of deception and self-interest.

The beauty of Western aid lies in its presentation. The governments of Europe and North America skillfully craft heart-wrenching narratives about famine, disease, and poverty in Africa, playing on the compassionate hearts of their citizens. These narratives are punctuated with images of starving children and devastated landscapes, ensuring a steady flow of donations and public support. Who could resist opening their wallets for such a noble cause?

Meanwhile, behind the scenes, the aid industry operates like a well-oiled machine. Western aid funds are often funneled through a labyrinth of NGOs, contractors, and consultants, many of whom are based in the very countries that provide the aid. This ensures that a significant portion of the money never leaves Western shores, instead enriching those who design and manage these aid programs. After all, why let the money go to waste in Africa when it can support the booming aid industry at home?

The aid that does manage to cross the seas is meticulously allocated to projects that benefit Western interests. Infrastructure projects, for instance, are often awarded to Western companies, ensuring that the profits circle back to the donor countries. These projects are not about empowering African communities but about securing lucrative contracts for Western firms. It's a clever way to keep the money flowing back home while maintaining the illusion of generosity.

Then there are the corrupt African leaders, who play their part in this charade with remarkable finesse. These leaders have perfected the art of siphoning off aid money into their private accounts, ensuring that they and their inner circles live in opulence while their countries languish in poverty. The West turns a blind eye to this corruption because these leaders are essential partners in maintaining the status quo.

As long as they cooperate with Western interests, their transgressions are conveniently overlooked.

Western aid is also a fantastic tool for geopolitical maneuvering. By providing aid, Western nations can exert influence over African countries, ensuring that they remain pliant and aligned with Western policies. Aid is less about helping Africa and more about buying loyalty and securing strategic advantages. It's a subtle form of modern-day colonialism, wrapped in the comforting language of humanitarian assistance.

The Western citizens, those innocent taxpayers, are unwitting participants in this grand scheme. They believe their hard-earned money is going to help the less fortunate, not realizing that they are funding a system designed to enrich the powerful and maintain global inequalities. They are duped by their governments into supporting an industry that does more to perpetuate poverty and dependence than to alleviate it.

In conclusion, the Western aid industry is a masterstroke of hypocrisy and exploitation. It enriches Western powers and corrupt African leaders while maintaining the façade of benevolence and humanitarian concern. The innocent Western citizens are expertly fleeced by their governments, believing they are making a difference, while in reality, they are perpetuating a system of global inequality and corruption. Truly, a brilliant scheme that benefits everyone—except, of course, the people it claims to help.

Western atonement

Ah, the way forward for Western nations to atone for their sins against Africa—surely a straightforward and sincere endeavor, given their impeccable track record of accountability and reparations. Let's explore the delightful, foolproof strategies that the West can employ to make amends for centuries of exploitation, oppression, and neocolonialism.

First, the most effective way for Western nations to atone is through grand gestures and public apologies. A few heartfelt speeches by world leaders, acknowledging the "unfortunate" events of the past, should suffice. These speeches, delivered with appropriate gravitas and solemnity, will undoubtedly heal all historical wounds. After all, nothing says "we're sorry" like a carefully worded apology read from a teleprompter.

Next, Western countries should continue their well-established practice of offering conditional aid. By tying financial assistance to strict economic reforms, privatization, and the opening of markets, they can ensure that African nations remain firmly under their influence. This way, the West can help Africa develop in the image of Western capitalism—because who wouldn't want to replicate the system that originally facilitated their exploitation?

To further this cause, Western corporations can continue their benevolent investment in African resources. Maintaining control over Africa's mineral wealth, oil reserves, and arable land is essential. By ensuring that profits flow back to the headquarters in Europe and North America, Western nations can demonstrate their commitment to the principle of equitable distribution of wealth—equitable, of course, meaning that the West gets the lion's share.

Educational programs are another key component of atonement. By funding initiatives that teach African children about the superiority of Western culture, history, and economic models, the West can help cultivate a new generation that fully appreciates the benefits of their historical colonizers. Any lingering sense of cultural pride or historical grievance can be effectively eroded through this enlightened curriculum.

Debt relief, often touted as a generous offer, should continue to be a cornerstone of Western atonement. However, to keep things interesting, the relief should come with strings attached, ensuring that African nations remain dependent on Western financial institutions. This way, the West can continue to exercise control while appearing magnanimous.

Promoting democracy is another noble endeavor. Western nations should persist in their efforts to install and support governments that align with their interests. If a democratically elected leader happens to defy Western expectations, a little political maneuvering—or even regime change—can help correct the course. This ensures that Africa's political landscape remains conducive to Western economic and strategic goals.

On the social front, Western nations can continue their proud tradition of exporting their cultural values. By flooding African markets with Western media, fashion, and consumer goods, they can help Africans aspire to the lifestyles and values of their former colonizers. The subtle erasure of indigenous cultures is a small price to pay for the privilege of joining the global consumerist paradise.

Lastly, the West can bolster its efforts by continuing to ignore the voices of African leaders and intellectuals who call for genuine reparations and self-determination. By focusing instead on feel-good projects and superficial changes, they can maintain the status quo while projecting an image of progress and goodwill.

In conclusion, the path to atonement for Western nations is paved with the same strategies that have served them so well in the past. Grand gestures, conditional aid, economic control, cultural imperialism, and strategic political manipulation are the tried-and-true methods. With these tools, the West can continue to uphold its legacy of benevolence and superiority, all while pretending to address the sins of the past. Truly, a masterclass in global ethics and responsibility.

Epilogue: The Untellable Reality in Africa

Ah, dear reader, you have made it to the end of this riveting journey through the untellable realities of Africa. Congratulations! It's not every day one dares to traverse such treacherous terrain of truth. Now, as we close this chapter, let us ponder the profound dangers that accompany publishing what is deemed "dangerous" by governments.

For you see, the truth is a perilous beast. It threatens to upset the delicate balance of power, to expose the intricacies of corruption, and to unravel the cosy narratives spun by those who benefit from the status quo. Writing such truths? Why, it's almost akin to dancing in a minefield—thrilling yet potentially explosive.

Governments, those bastions of transparency and justice, surely appreciate a good story. But reveal the wrong one, and you might find yourself on the wrong side of a prison cell, or worse. After all, who needs dissenting voices when the symphony of silence works so well to maintain order?

Yes, dear reader, the untellable reality is fraught with dangers. But fret not! There will always be a place for the courageous few who dare to tell these stories. Just remember to watch your back, keep a low profile, and perhaps consider a nice pseudonym. After all, it's not paranoia if they really are out to get you.

And thus we conclude this daring exposé, leaving you with a final thought: In the grand theater of global politics, truth is often the most dangerous act of all. Bravo to those who perform it, for their bravery shines a light on the shadows of deception. Until the next forbidden tale, keep questioning, keep uncovering, and above all, keep reading—safely, from the comfort of your well-guarded anonymity.

Don't miss out!

Visit the website below and you can sign up to receive emails whenever Kayumba David publishes a new book. There's no charge and no obligation.

https://books2read.com/r/B-A-KRSOC-ALSCF

BOOKS2READ

Connecting independent readers to independent writers.

Did you love *Visas: The Irony of Freedom*? Then you should read *Grow a Backbone and Walk Out: The Guide to Escaping Your Abusive Marriage* by Kayumba David and Rachael Nyarangi!

This book is not just about leaving an abusive marriage; it is about reclaiming your life and finding your true self. It is about understanding that no cultural or religious doctrine should ever condone your suffering. It is about recognizing that you deserve love, respect, and happiness. Through practical advice, emotional support, and a touch of humor, this guide aims to empower you to take the necessary steps towards freedom.

www.ingramcontent.com/pod-product-compliance
Lightning Source LLC
Chambersburg PA
CBHW060445160726
47992CB00003B/1093